Exquisite Creatures

THE INSECT ART OF CHRISTOPHER MARLEY

Pomegranate

SAN FRANCISCO

Pomegranate Communications, Inc.
Box 808022, Petaluma CA 94975
800-227-1428
www.pomegranate.com

Pomegranate Europe Ltd.
Unit 1, Heathcote Business Centre, Hurlbutt Road
Warwick, Warwickshire CV34 6TD, UK
[+44] 0 1926 430111

ISBN 0-7649-3217-9
Pomegranate Catalog No. AA278

Pomegranate publishes books of
postcards on a wide range of subjects.
Please contact the publisher for more information.

Cover designed by Lisa Reid
Printed in China
14 13 12 11 10 09 08 07 06 05   10 9 8 7 6 5 4 3 2 1

To facilitate detachment of the postcards from this book, fold each card along its perforation line before tearing.

*P*erhaps no organisms on earth evoke such visceral emotions as insects. From the delight of a close-up encounter with a tiger swallowtail to the horror of an invasion of roaches, insects have the power to move us, both emotionally and literally. Christopher Marley is devoted to fostering a human reaction to insects that is perhaps left wanting—awe. In his artwork, a sleek, symmetrical style is juxtaposed with the most organic of subject matter, resulting in a macrocosm of color, texture, and form. The resulting dichotomy puts insects in a new light. Arthropods viewed through Marley's lens lose their creeping, scuttling ominousness, leaving only the wonder that such color could exist—nearly undiscovered—in nature, that such expeditious, functional design could ever have gone unappreciated.

As with most people, Marley's original emotion toward most insects was, frankly, fear. As a young artist, his subject matter of choice was always the fantastical and the macabre, but the prospect of a big "bug" was practically paralyzing. This condition was not lessened when Marley began traveling at the age of 19. A couple of years in South America greeted him with much fodder to feed his phobia, and several years in Southeast Asia and Africa were not much better. One night in a Bangkok artisan market, Marley stumbled upon a group of people selling what he thought were small marsupials crammed into cheap frames. On closer examination, he recognized them as insects. The ensuing horror was accompanied by a new and wholly unexpected emotion: a surging fascination. As he examined these specimens, he was enthralled with their size, colors, outlandish shapes, and perfect mechanics. Years of study of entomology followed, then excursions to remote locales to collect and observe prized species in their native habitat. Finally came the blending of this obsession with Marley's work as an artist.

Marley's passion for insects does not end with their use as a medium of design. Some of the world's most remarkable insects, such as Queen Alexandra's birdwing—the largest butterfly, with a wingspan of nearly 12 inches—are threatened or endangered. Marley agrees with the assertion of many leading entomologists and conservation organizations that a greater appreciation of insects through collection, study, and artwork can actually aid in their preservation. Given that destruction of habitat or host plant is the only real threat to the vast majority of insect species, the foremost effort in their conservation must be preservation of the grasslands, forests, and jungles where they dwell. Once there is an increased appreciation for these unknown treasures, an economic incentive can be proffered in the form of an already existing "crop"—beautiful insects—marketable to collectors, naturalists, artists, educators, and the like. The habitat thus becomes more valuable in its relatively untouched condition than it would be if it were developed.

Exquisite Creatures
THE INSECT ART OF CHRISTOPHER MARLEY

African blue swallowtail *(Papilio zalmoxis)* from Mongoumba, Central Africa, wingspan approximately 16 cm (6⁵⁄₁₆ in.).

BOX 808022   PETALUMA   CA 94975

Pomegranate

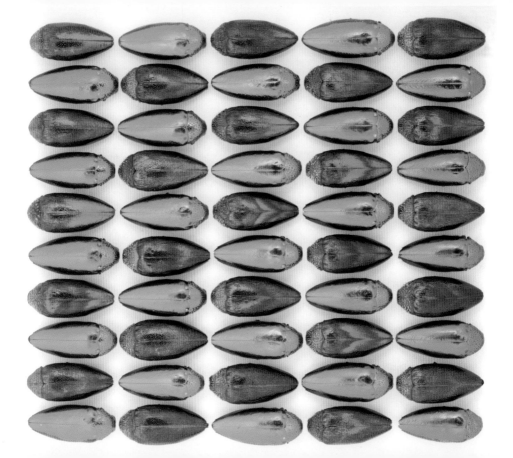

Exquisite Creatures
THE INSECT ART OF CHRISTOPHER MARLEY

Metallic wood-boring beetles—*Sternocera pulchra* (blue and purple) and *S. ruficornis* (green)—from Tanzania and Thailand, respectively, 40 mm (1⁹⁄₁₆ in.) long.

BOX 808022   PETALUMA   CA 94975

Pomegranate

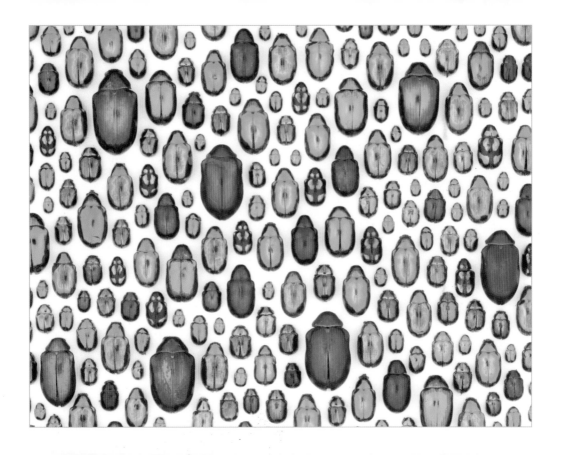

Exquisite Creatures
THE INSECT ART OF CHRISTOPHER MARLEY

Leaf beetles of the family Chrysomelidae, subfamily Eumolpinae, from Thailand and Java, 3–8 mm (⅛–5/16 in.) long.

BOX 808022   PETALUMA   CA 94975

Pomegranate

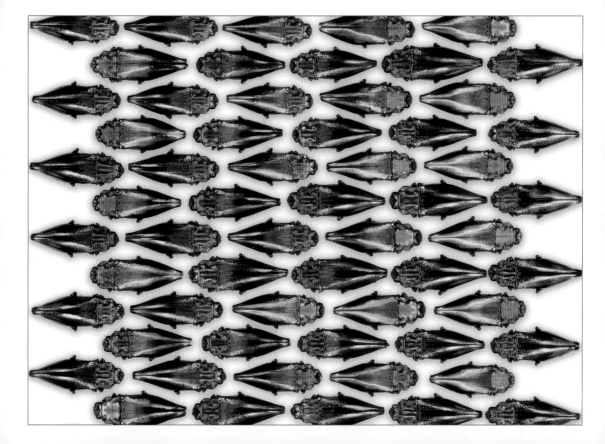

Exquisite Creatures
THE INSECT ART OF CHRISTOPHER MARLEY

Metallic wood-boring beetles (*Chrysodema* sp.) from Fak Fak, Irian
Jaya, Indonesia, 30 mm ($^{13}/_{16}$ in.) long.

Pomegranate

BOX 808022   PETALUMA   CA 94975

Exquisite Creatures

THE INSECT ART OF CHRISTOPHER MARLEY

Giant blues *(Arhopala hercules)* from Papua and Indonesia, wingspan
more than 5 cm (2 in.).

BOX 808022   PETALUMA   CA 94975

Pomegranate

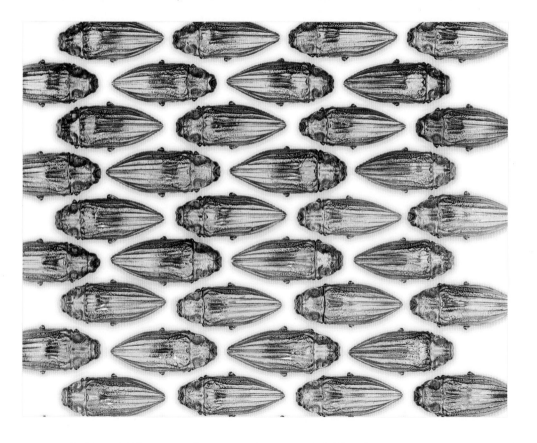

Exquisite Creatures

THE INSECT ART OF CHRISTOPHER MARLEY

Metallic wood-boring beetles *(Cyphogastra javanica)* from Kei Kecil,
Dulah Island, Indonesia, 37 mm (1⁷⁄₁₆ in.) long.

Pomegranate BOX 808022 PETALUMA CA 94975

Exquisite Creatures
THE INSECT ART OF CHRISTOPHER MARLEY

Metallic wood-boring beetles *(Belionota tricolor)* from Seram Island,
Indonesia, 27–30 mm (1¹/₁₆–1³/₁₆ in.) long.

BOX 808022   PETALUMA   CA 94975

Pomegranate

Exquisite Creatures
THE INSECT ART OF CHRISTOPHER MARLEY

Frog beetles *(Sagra buqueti)* from the Cameroun Highlands of
Malaysia, 27–30 mm (1¹⁄₁₆–1³⁄₁₆ in.) long.

BOX 808022   PETALUMA   CA 94975

Pomegranate

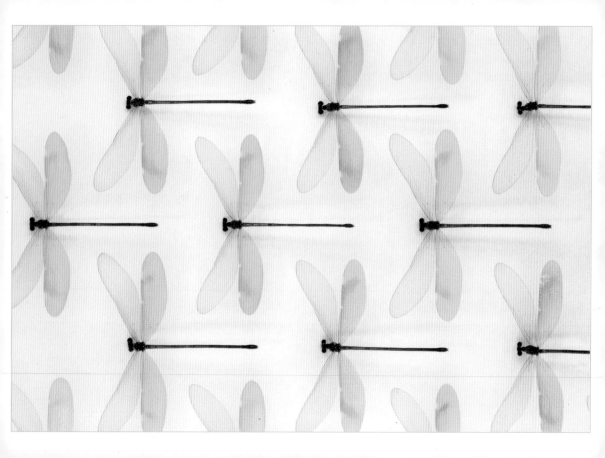

Exquisite Creatures

THE INSECT ART OF CHRISTOPHER MARLEY

Damselflies (order Odonata) from Malaysia, wingspan 7 cm (2¾ in.).

Pomegranate

BOX 808022 PETALUMA CA 94975

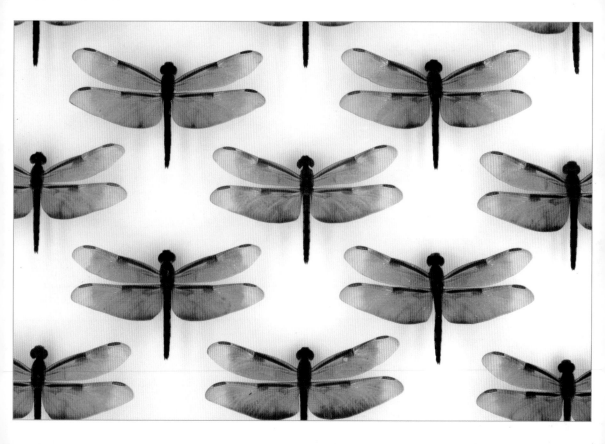

Exquisite Creatures

THE INSECT ART OF CHRISTOPHER MARLEY

Dragonflies (order Odonata) from Chiang Mai, Thailand,
wingspan 5.5 cm (2³/₁₆ in.).

Pomegranate

BOX 808022   PETALUMA   CA 94975

Exquisite Creatures
THE INSECT ART OF CHRISTOPHER MARLEY

Brimstone butterflies *(Gonepteryx rhamni)* from Macedonia,
wingspan 5 cm (2 in.).

BOX 808022 PETALUMA CA 94975

Pomegranate

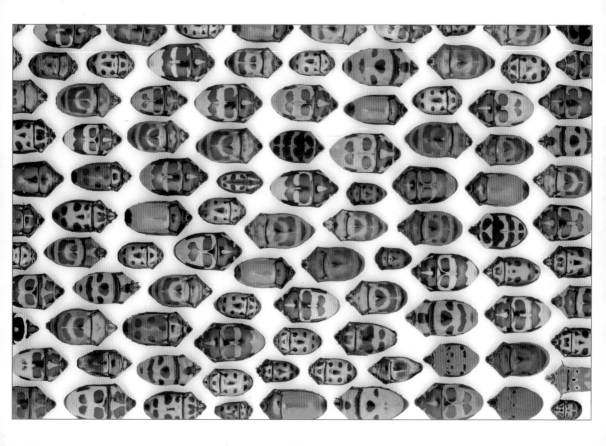

Exquisite Creatures
THE INSECT ART OF CHRISTOPHER MARLEY

Shield-backed bugs of the family Scutelleridae from Madagascar, Java,
Uganda, Thailand, and Irian Jaya, 12–20 mm (½–¹³⁄₁₆ in.) long.

Pomegranate

BOX 808022   PETALUMA   CA 94975

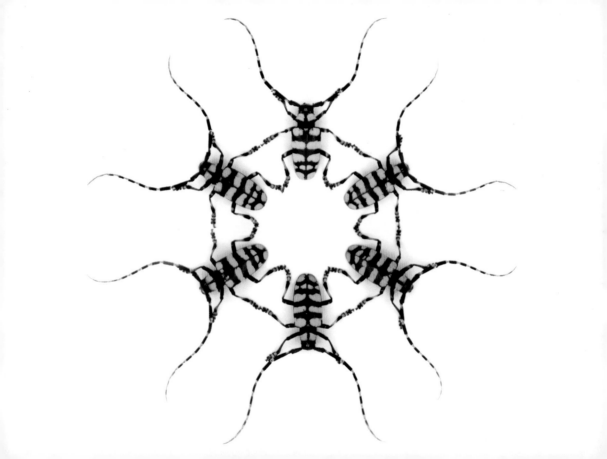

Exquisite Creatures
THE INSECT ART OF CHRISTOPHER MARLEY

Longhorn beetles *(Anoplophora elegans)* from Chiang Rai, Thailand, 4.5 cm (1¾ in.) long.

BOX 808022   PETALUMA   CA 94975

Pomegranate

Exquisite Creatures
THE INSECT ART OF CHRISTOPHER MARLEY

Shining leaf beetles (family Scarabaeidae, subfamily Rutelinae) from
Venezuela, Costa Rica, Guatemala, Japan, Indonesia, Australia,
Argentina, Thailand, and the United States, 15–35 mm (⁹⁄₁₆–1⅜ in.)
long.

Pomegranate

BOX 808022   PETALUMA   CA 94975

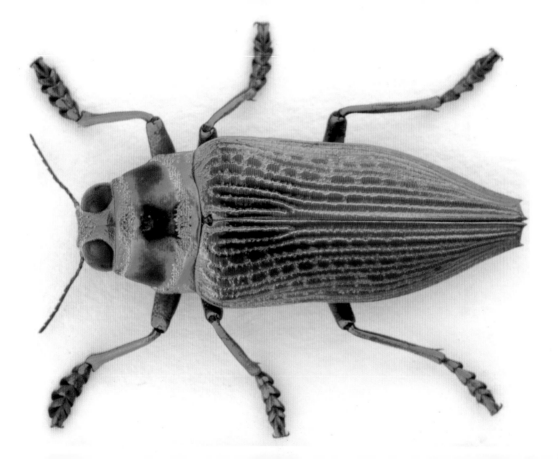

Exquisite Creatures
THE INSECT ART OF CHRISTOPHER MARLEY

Brazilian wood-boring beetle *(Psiloptera bicarinata)* from Amazonas,
Brazil, 4 cm (1 9/16 in.) long.

Pomegranate

BOX 808022 PETALUMA CA 94975

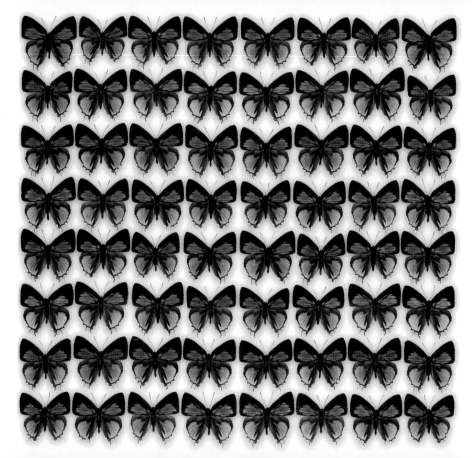

Exquisite Creatures
THE INSECT ART OF CHRISTOPHER MARLEY

Philippine blues (*Arhopala* sp.) from Mindanao, Philippines,
wingspan 3.5 cm (1⅜ in.).

Pomegranate

BOX 808022   PETALUMA   CA 94975

Exquisite Creatures
THE INSECT ART OF CHRISTOPHER MARLEY

Metallic wood-boring beetles (family Buprestidae), shining leaf
scarabs (family Scarabaeidae, subfamily Rutelinae), tortoise beetles
and leaf beetles (family Chrysomelidae), and ladybird beetles (family
Coccinellidae) from Indonesia, France, Australia, and Thailand,
3–45 mm (⅛–1¾ in.) long.

BOX 808022   PETALUMA   CA 94975

Pomegranate

Exquisite Creatures
THE INSECT ART OF CHRISTOPHER MARLEY

Morpho butterflies from Bolivia *(M. godarti)* and Peru (*M. didius pseudogodarti* and *M. didius*), wingspan 14 cm (5½ in.).

Pomegranate

BOX 808022 PETALUMA CA 94975

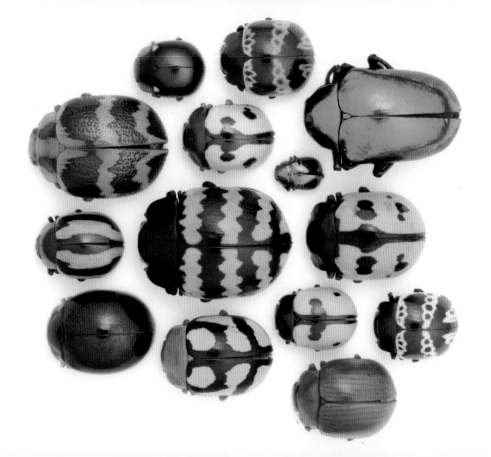

Exquisite Creatures
THE INSECT ART OF CHRISTOPHER MARLEY

Leaf beetles of the family Chrysomelidae, subfamily Chrysomelinae,
from Peru, 6–22 mm (¼–⅞ in.) long.

BOX 808022   PETALUMA   CA 94975

Pomegranate

Exquisite Creatures

THE INSECT ART OF CHRISTOPHER MARLEY

Morpho sulkowski from the Andes of Bolivia and Peru, wingspan almost 9 cm (3%16 in.).

Pomegranate

BOX 808022   PETALUMA   CA 94975

Exquisite Creatures
THE INSECT ART OF CHRISTOPHER MARLEY

Weevils (family Curculionidae) from New Guinea, Brazil, and
Indonesia, 1.75–3 cm ($^{11}/_{16}$–1$^{3}/_{16}$ in.) long.

BOX 808022   PETALUMA   CA 94975

Pomegranate

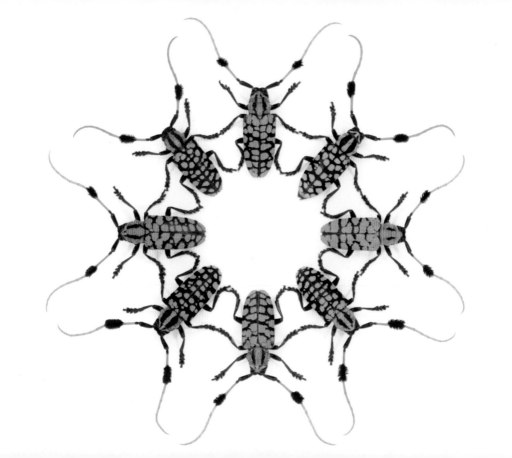

Exquisite Creatures
THE INSECT ART OF CHRISTOPHER MARLEY

Longhorn beetles *(Aristobia approximator)* from Chiang Mai,
Thailand, 2.5 cm (1 in.) long, excluding antennae.

BOX 808022   PETALUMA   CA 94975

Pomegranate

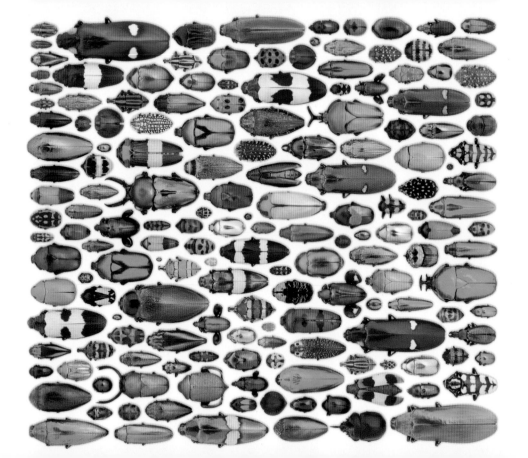

Exquisite Creatures
THE INSECT ART OF CHRISTOPHER MARLEY

Various beetles (order Coleoptera) from Malaysia, Thailand,
Indonesia, Madagascar, Australia, Peru, and France, 6–45 mm
(¼–1 ¾ in.) long.

BOX 808022   PETALUMA   CA 94975

Pomegranate

Exquisite Creatures
THE INSECT ART OF CHRISTOPHER MARLEY

Jeweled weevil *(Lamprocyphus augustus)* from Rondonia, Brazil,
30 mm (1³⁄₁₆ in.) long.

Pomegranate

BOX 808022   PETALUMA   CA 94975

Exquisite Creatures
THE INSECT ART OF CHRISTOPHER MARLEY

Morpho aurora butterfly subspecies—*M. aurora aurora* (subtle opalescent blue) and *M. aurora aureola* (deeper blue)—from Bolivia and Peru, respectively, wingspan 8.5 cm (3⅜ in.).

Pomegranate

BOX 808022   PETALUMA   CA 94975

Exquisite Creatures
THE INSECT ART OF CHRISTOPHER MARLEY

Beetles (order Coleoptera) and bugs (Hemiptera) from North
and South America, Europe, Asia, Africa, and Australia, 3–75 mm
(⅛–3 in.) long.

BOX 808022 PETALUMA CA 94975

Pomegranate

Exquisite Creatures
THE INSECT ART OF CHRISTOPHER MARLEY

Tropical cracker butterflies *(Hamadryas velutina)* from Peru,
wingspan 6 cm (2⅜ in.).

BOX 808022   PETALUMA   CA 94975

Pomegranate

Exquisite Creatures
THE INSECT ART OF CHRISTOPHER MARLEY

Morpho helena butterfly from Tingo Maria, Peru, wingspan 14 cm (5½ in.).

Pomegranate

BOX 808022   PETALUMA   CA 94975

Exquisite Creatures
THE INSECT ART OF CHRISTOPHER MARLEY

Clearwing butterflies *(Cithaerias pyropina)* from Iquitos, Peru,
wingspan 5.5 cm (2³⁄₁₆ in.).

BOX 808022   PETALUMA   CA 94975

Pomegranate

Exquisite Creatures
THE INSECT ART OF CHRISTOPHER MARLEY

Leaf beetle (*Doryphora* sp.) from Venezuela, 2 cm (13/16 in.) long.

Pomegranate

BOX 808022 PETALUMA CA 94975